GRANDMA (ALMOST) BECOMES QUEEN

Alison Grunwald

WHAT THEY'RE SAYING ABOUT
Grandma (Almost) Becomes Queen

A hilarious story that had the class laughing out loud. My class particularly loved hearing Grandma's song. I loved the way it wove the history of the Tudors with a modern-day granny. I highly recommend this book for all children of primary age.
Bianca, Year 3 Teacher and Curriculum Development Lead

I loved the part where Grandma disappears into thin air. It's a very exciting story — Grandma's very adventurous, and the jokes are funny.
Hannah, 10

The cartoons really made the story come to life.
Salma, 9

It made history fun and exciting. The pictures are funny. Any age group will find the jokes funny – even parents!

Haruna, 9

I enjoyed learning about the history of the Windsor family. It was really funny, and I understood the vocabulary!

Eriny, 10

I loved the story – my favourite part was the singing – Grandma's voice was like a squeaky bicycle!

Libi, 8

I find it funny that Grandma always misunderstands Gertrude…I don't think Gertrude likes Grandma.

Louis, 7

I loved Grandma telling funny jokes that King Henry didn't get!

Clara, 8

Copyright © 2023 by Alison Grunwald
All rights reserved.
www.alisongrunwald.co.uk

No part of this book may be reproduced in any form or by any electronic or mechanical means, including information storage and retrieval systems, without written permission from the author, except for the use of brief quotations in a book review.

Illustration by Mike Phillips (Beehive Illustration).

With thanks to literary consultant Claire Wingfield for her invaluable help.

Published by Blue Robin Press.

Robins are loved for their beauty, speed and bravery. They are also rather cunning and will dart in to steal a meal from a much larger bird when it is not looking! They are mischievous, just like Grandma in these stories, and they can't resist having a bit of fun.

We wondered what disguise a robin might use if it did not want to be noticed, and the answer seemed obvious: it would mix up some blue poster paint and jump right in. Who would recognise a blue robin?

Imagine what crazy tricks it could get up to!

With love to little princesses Chloe Rose
and Zoe Rosa

WHATEVER NEXT, GRANDMA!

CONTENTS

1. Off to Windsor 1
2. Do shut up, Grandma! 4
3. Castle Magic 8
4. What's The Time? 13
5. "I'm Henry Tudor, your King" 16
6. "Bring the Cat" 21
7. Grandma Behaves Badly 25
8. Gertrude's Great Escape 30
9. "I'm Just Grandma" 34

About the Author 38
What's Gertrude Made of? 42
Answers 44

1

OFF TO WINDSOR

MY Grandma loves reading History books that tell you what happened a long time ago.

For instance, did you know that birds used to be dinosaurs, that pancakes were invented two thousand years ago, and that Queen Victoria was Queen Elizabeth II's great, great grandma?

In Victorian times ladies hid their knees, wearing swishy dresses down to the ground. Gentlemen wore black high hats, just like the Mad Hatter in *Alice in Wonderland*!

ALISON GRUNWALD

Grandma read that kings and queens sometimes lived in a place called Windsor and that our Royal Family are called Windsor.

So it was on a bright May morning that my Grandma resolved to visit Windsor Great Park, home to delicate red deer and the famous Windsor Castle. She loved train journeys and this was the perfect day for one.

Dressing herself in her best gold onesie, finished off with a shiny cowboy hat and purple cowboy boots, Grandma smiled at her reflection in the mirror. "Yes indeed," she said, approvingly.

"Come along, Gertrude. No time to lie around…we're going to Windsor for the day," she announced. And with no time to argue, Gertrude found herself locked firmly into her wicker travel basket and on her way to the train station.

2

DO SHUT UP, GRANDMA

GRANDMA was in a good mood; she had a feeling great things were about to happen and she was excited. She started to sing in a high, scratchy voice: "My bonny lies over the ocean... my bonny lies over the sea... my bonny lies over the ocean........ oh bring back my bonny to meee."

"Oh help. LET MIAOWT!" yelled Gertrude, desperately.

This rarely worked, and it did not work today.

Grandma was delighted! "Yes, you can join in, Gertrude," she grinned, mistaking the cat's loud miaow for pleasure. "Here comes the chorus!"

And she was off again...

"Bring back, oh bring back, oh bring back my bonny to meee to meee.

Bring back, oh bring back, oh bring back my bonny to meee," she rasped, her voice sounding like chalk on a blackboard.

As she often did, Gertrude tried to open the basket with her sharp little teeth to make a run for it, but Grandma knew that trick well and had secured the door tightly with a strong piece of string. "Settle down, Gertrude."

She launched herself into the second verse, her voice now sounding like a saw, sawing wood.

"Last night as I lay on my pillow
Last night as I lay on my bed,
I stuck my feet out of the window
And now all my neighbours have fled."

"Oh do shut up!" miaowed Gertude, her paws so deep in her ears they almost met in the middle. But Grandma was building up to her grand finale. She was not put off by Gertrude's miaows, which, as usual, she mistook for approval. Taking a deep breath, she yodelled:

"Bring back, oh bring back
Oh bring back my neighbours to

meee, to meee.
Bring back, oh bring **BAAACK**
Oh bring back my neighbours to meee."

3

CASTLE MAGIC

THE rest of the train ride to Windsor passed peacefully as my Grandma was reading a book on King Henry VIII, which took a lot of concentration. She was amazed to discover that often people didn't have a bath for months in Tudor times – they must have ponged badly, she thought.

GRANDMA (ALMOST) BECOMES QUEEN

Gertrude managed a nice nap before the travel basket was whisked up into the air and they were on the move once again.

Windsor Castle was twinkling in the distance like the magic turrets at Disneyland, and the great park opened before them – glorious flowers, ancient cedar trees and red deer dotting the landscape. It was magnificent.

As Grandma began striding towards a copse of leafy oak trees a very strange and wonderful thing occurred: the air around her and Gertrude seemed to shimmer, and there was a crackling sound, a bit like when you scrunch aluminium foil up into a ball.

Grandma continued walking towards the trees when, as if by magic, they flickered into the distance, and disappeared!

Barely a second later the pair found themselves on a different hillside, yet still within sight of Windsor Castle.

An even odder thing had happened: as Grandma looked down, she noticed that her clothes had changed. Instead of her gold outfit and purple cowboy boots she was now wearing a gorgeous, velvet dress. A smart black bodice laced tight against her chest sat above the skirt, falling in shiny, ruby-red folds to the ground.

She glanced at her right foot and gasped! The purple boots had vanished into thin air.

In their place was a gleaming pair of green silk shoes, resplendent with pointy toes and little satin heels.

Feeling for her frizzy red hair, Grandma gasped again! It was no longer frizzy, but smooth and sleek, a soft white linen cap perched neatly on the top of her head, trailing a gauzy flounce down to her bare shoulders. Goodness gracious... Grandma had become a Tudor lady! Even Gertrude wore a crisp white ruff around the soft fur of her neck.

4

WHAT'S THE TIME?

WHAT on earth had happened to them? Had they somehow gone back in time? How?

Grandma remembered the shimmering crackle and a startling thought popped into her mind: somehow she and Gertrude must have stepped through a hidden gate – a sort of time warp. It was now 500 years in the past...they were in History!

Another thought closely followed on. If they were 500 years in the past, how would they get back to the present day? Would they be stuck in

Tudor England forever? It was a scary notion.

An oddly familiar sound floated on the breeze towards them. It sounded a bit like a trumpet, but not quite. Grandma racked her brains...oh yes, she was sure it was a horn.

"**Too-toot, too-tooot. Too-toot, too-tooot**," it went.

The notes reminded Grandma of something else: now what was it?

It suddenly came to her: this was the sound made by huntsmen, on the trail of a fox!

In a flash there they were...a stampede of colourfully dressed huntsmen on horses, chasing a pack of yelping foxhounds. And they were heading in her direction.

"Gertrude, what do I do?" hissed my Grandma, staring wide-eyed at the approaching horsemen.

5

"I'M HENRY TUDOR, YOUR KING"

THE one in the lead was tallest – and plumpest; he was galloping full-tilt towards them, the sound of the horses' hooves building to a drumming crescendo.

Gertrude had a bad feeling and tried to hide under the scratchy ruff. She covered her eyes with her tail.

Grandma was also sure she was about about to be run over and shielded her face with a velvet arm.

The noise of the horses' hooves became even more thunderous and Grandma clutched Gertrude's basket tightly, and started to pray.

"MADAM!" boomed a deep voice from above her. "Do you realise you are on private Windsor property, and you have intruded most impolite on our morning sport?"

"What did he mean?" thought Grandma to herself but wisely not saying anything to the red-faced man.

"Madam, pray take your sleeve away from your nose and do me the courtesy of looking at me when I address you," he instructed.

"Look up Grandma!" miaowed Gertrude, urgently.

Grandma raised her eyes and looked at the man on the horse, which was now stamping on the ground irritably with its hoof, eager to be on its way.

"What is your name, pray?" was

the huntsman's next question.

Grandma wondered about all this praying. But remaining silent was not going to get her out of this fix; she knew she had to say something. What was a good Tudor name? Her mind flew back to the history book she had been reading that morning.

"Katherine," declared Grandma, as firmly as she dared.

"Ah, that is a name I know well," smiled the man on the horse. "Sooth, you are...comely," he added, his face blushing even more pink.

"What is *your* name?" enquired my Grandma boldly, wondering what 'comely' meant.

"Henry," replied the huntsman.

"Henry Tudor...I am your King!"

ALISON GRUNWALD

"Crikey," was Gertrude's first thought.

"This isn't good," was her second.

"Pray, madam, tell me," said the King, a cunning gleam in his eye. "Are you a *married* lady?"

"No, sire. A widow lady," replied my Grandma, suddenly understanding whom she was talking to. She remembered something rather worrying about this King Henry. It was a rhyme about his many wives that she had learnt many years ago in school. It went something like this:

"Divorced, beheaded, died.
Divorced, beheaded, survived."

6

"BRING THE CAT"

KING HENRY VIII had married six ladies and was always greedily on the lookout for another wife. Some of them hadn't done so well, Grandma recalled; it was rather hard to manage without your head, after all.

Glancing at the King again left her in no doubt that the man on the horse was, indeed, Henry VIII. She had seen a painting of him in Cricklewood public library!

GRANDMA (ALMOST) BECOMES QUEEN

"Well, Sire, I thought I was widowed, but I'm not really sure," she stammered, hoping Henry would be put off.

The amorous King was not deterred. "Madam, you seem uncertain whether you have a husband or not. While you are thinking on it, pray join me tonight for our May Feast. My castle is your castle. Bring the cat, too."

With that, the hunting party galloped off down the hillside leaving a little cloud of dust in their wake.

"Oh crumbs, what should I do, Gertrude?" hissed my Grandma. She was in deep trouble as this King was the very same one who got rid of his wives when he was fed up with them. There was obviously a vacancy.

GRANDMA (ALMOST) BECOMES QUEEN

Grandma had read all about Henry, and the story did not have a happy ending. Whatever happened she must not agree to marry him – he was too unpredictable.

7

GRANDMA BEHAVES BADLY

THAT evening Grandma hit on a plan: she would behave very badly at the castle.

Gertrude could hiss and spit: that was bound to make a bad impression. But Grandma's scheme got off to a bad start.

"You are smelly and revolting," she told the King, rudely, crinkling up her nose.

"Ah sweet madam, you jest," chuckled Henry VIII.

"I'm NOT joking."

Grandma was beginning to feel exasperated when another idea suddenly popped into her head...

GRANDMA (ALMOST) BECOMES QUEEN

If she told really BAD jokes – maybe they would put Henry off her! There was only one way to find out.

"Sire, can I tell you a few jokes?" Grandma smiled, sweetly.

"Lady you pulleth my leg, but I like it," replied Henry, flirtatiously.

Grandma began with an easy one. "Why was the king so busy at school?" she asked Henry.

"No clue," shrugged Henry VIII. "Tell me, madam."

"Because he had so many subjects," Grandma replied. Gertrude groaned: she'd heard that one before.

The King looked unimpressed. Grandma tried again...

"What kind of king comes from Denmark?" she asked.

"No idea! What kind of king comes from Denmark?" repeated Henry.

"A Viking!"

Grandma hardly paused for breath. The King looked bored, which was good!

"What kind of king can you use in maths?"

"You've got me," shrugged Henry. He wasn't much good at adding up.

"A 30cm ruler," Grandma replied,

grinning.

The King looked confused, wondering what 30cm meant. Gertrude wasn't sure either.

"I think we're winning, Gertrude," whispered Grandma, excitedly. She had one more really bad joke to tell the King that she was certain would put him off her for good. It was now or never.

"Why couldn't the king stop jumping?" she asked, staring hard into Henry's eyes.

"Lady, I couldn't say. Why couldn't the king stop jumping?"

"Because he lived in a bouncy castle," Grandma quipped, not expecting King Henry to get it.

She was wrong.

ALISON GRUNWALD

8

GERTRUDE'S GREAT ESCAPE

"TERRIFIC, lady!" shouted the King, collapsing sideways onto the table and overturning a large bowl of trifle. He was shaking with laughter, his guffaws ringing round the wood-panelled feasting hall.

"Madam, I adore you," he whispered, nuzzling Grandma's left ear.

"Carry on teasing me...do."

Grandma realised there was only one thing for it, but it was a huge gamble. She turned to the King and managed a flirtatious wink.

"Sire, I am going to take some air

in the gardens. Come out to join me... soon."

This was the most dangerous joke she had ever played on anyone, and if it went wrong she and Gertrude might find themselves imprisoned in the Tower of London. If only she could find the magic portal in time, she would never have to look at horrible Henry VIII again. She would be free. She opened Gertrude's travel basket and let her out.

Gertrude understood and sprinted off down the hill into the park, Grandma puffing behind and holding her heavy velvet dress up above her knees. Then her heart sank.

"**WAIT** madam. **STOP** I say." It was the lovesick King – and he was running fast towards them, his plump legs quivering in tan-coloured breeches.

ALISON GRUNWALD

"Quick, Gertrude…HOME!" yelled Grandma, picking up speed. But the King was still gaining, fast.

"HALT…IN THE NAME OF THE KING," screeched Henry, buttons pinging off his velvet jacket in all directions, one landing with a bonk on Gertrude's head.

Grandma's eyes were fixed on the nimble black-and-white cat, her breath coming in gasps.

Gertrude abruptly vanished into thin air, just as King Henry made a cheeky grab for Grandma. But the King's hands slapped together emptily, for Grandma was suddenly not where she was meant to be. She had disappeared like a puff of smoke, right in front of him.

"Ye gads," yelled Henry VIII in shock. "The lady vanishes!"

9

"I'M JUST GRANDMA"

THE next instant Gertrude and Grandma found themselves rolling over and over on the soft grass of a flat expanse of countryside but with no hills in sight. Windsor Castle still sparkled in the sunshine but, thankfully, no kings, horses or hounds could be seen anywhere.

"Gertrude you're a wonder," wheezed Grandma, completely out of breath.

"You found the time-portal...and just in time!" She hugged her furry friend tightly and kissed the tip of her cold little nose.

"Yuk," said Gertrude. *"MIAOW!"*

Looking down, Grandma found to her surprise that she was still wearing the Tudor dress, white cap and pointy shoes.

They received some very perplexed looks from the other passengers on the train journey back to Cricklewood, but my Grandma was too relieved to care. They had escaped!

Another joke suddenly flashed unbidden into her mind.

"Why was the monarch so lazy?" she asked Gertrude.

"I dunno. Why was the monarch so lazy?" miaowed the cat.

"Because he was the Lie-in King!" Grandma chortled.

"Oh that's terrible," Gertrude groaned.

The ticket collector couldn't resist a joke himself, when the oddly dressed pair arrived.

"Why, welcome back your Royal

Highness," he said, winking at my Grandma.

"And you, princess," he added, grinning at Gertrude, still in her white Tudor ruff.

"I'm nobody's Highness," snapped back Grandma. "I'm just Grandma. And that's who I'm planning to stay!"

ABOUT THE AUTHOR

A Londoner, Alison Grunwald has always loved writing comic stories and poems for children. She enjoyed working in primary schools teaching early reading to children arriving from other countries. One of the ways she did this was by inventing and singing a rap which made them laugh and helped them learn vowel sounds!

Alison has been a radio and

newspaper reporter and a doula. This is someone who looks after mums when they are expecting a baby and helps them learn how to feed and look after it. Sometimes twins arrive and Alison knows what to do because she has twins herself!

These days, Alison has lots of grandchildren to help with suggestions for her funny stories.

You can get in touch with Alison at: **a.grunwald@btinternet.com** to send your stories, jokes or just to say hello. (Please get permission from a grown-up before sending your email.)

If you enjoyed this book, look out for more of Grandma and Gertrude's adventures. Visit Alison's website at: **www.alisongrunwald.co.uk** for more hilarious animal stories and activities. You might like to write a special book review for Amazon (ask for help if you need to). For now until next time, it's lots of love from Alison, Grandma, and of course Gertrude!

If you enjoy writing stories, here are a few tips to help you along.

- Decide what the tale is about.

- Find a comfortable place to write or type.

- Build your story with plenty of interest.

- Use great descriptions of your characters and setting.

- Remember to end your tale as well as it started. We all love a good ending!

HOW MANY HIDDEN WORDS CAN YOU FIND IN GERTRUDE'S NAME?

Can you find 15 words hidden in the word

GERTRUDE

?

There are a few more, but some are quite tricky so you may need to grab an adult!

Answers on the next page

ANSWERS

greed	deer	reed
dug	red	greet
tree	due	rug

rude

duet

true

get

rut

truer

edge

urge

gut

tug

Also

regret, egret, rued, tee, trudge, urged, turd, deter, dreg, err, erred, ruder, drug, rue.

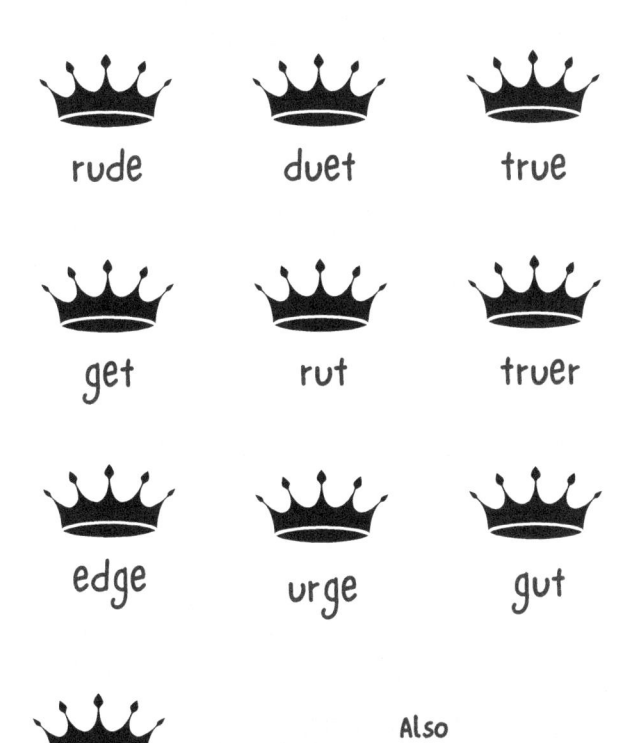

ALSO BY
ALISON GRUNWALD

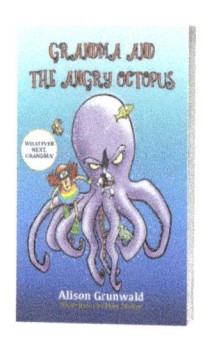

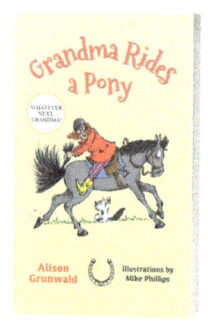

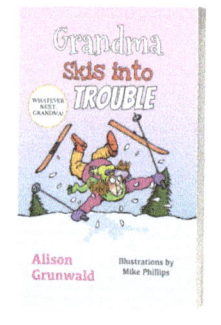

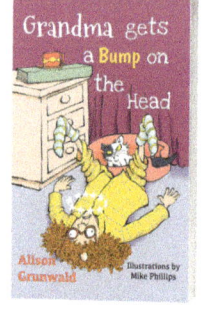

Watch out for

Grandma Goes to the Moon

Coming Soon!

Ingram Content Group UK Ltd.
Milton Keynes UK
UKHW020659290323
419307UK00010B/126